WORLD CUP action — Italy v. England in Rome in November 1976. Mick Mills has just cut off a pass to Causio

Andy Gray, Aston Villa's exciting striker

THE ALL STARS FOOTBALL BOOK NO. 17

edited by
COLIN TODD

with special contributions by
J. M. JEFFERY
STAN LIVERSEDGE
MIKE LYONS
LOU MACARI
JOE ROYLE
HARRY STANLEY
COLIN TODD
JOHN TOSHACK
JOHN TUDOR

WORLD DISTRIBUTORS, PUBLISHERS, LONDON

CONTENTS

© 1977 by Euro-Features Ltd/
World Distributors
Publishers, London
(A Member of the Pentos Group)
J. M. Jeffery, Stan Liversedge
Mike Lyons, Lou Macari
Joe Royle, Harry Stanley
Colin Todd, John Toshack
John Tudor.
All rights reserved.
First published by
World Distributors, Publishers, London

Printed in Spain.
SBN 7235 0435 0

Ray Clemence in action for Liverpool

There'll be Some Changes Made – by COLIN TODD

Colin Todd (right) in action for Derby against Q.P.R.

This is the sixth time when, about half way through our football season, I settle down to pen my editorial for ALL STARS. Often, as regular readers may have noticed, I have struck a personal note that filled in what had happened between the time of writing and the end of the season.

I remember well what had happened between the time I first wrote as editor of ALL STARS after taking over from Jim Armfield, and when the season finished and ALL STARS was published. What happened was simply that Derby County, whilst most people were looking to a photo-finish between Leeds, Liverpool and Manchester City, had come through to collect the Football League Championship!

And the same situation arose after I had written my editorial for the 1976 Annual. Then I noted that, with most clubs having about

twelve more matches to play, only seven points separated the top thirteen clubs in the First Division. Stoke and Burnley were leading the field, Derby were in seventh place. And it was Derby who, for the second time in four seasons, won the Championship.

Yet, as I wrote a year ago, the first half of the 1975–76 season brought two big disappointments—England's failure to qualify for the quarter-finals of the European Football Championship, and Derby's still surprising elimination from the European Champions Cup by Real Madrid. Surprising, not because Real are ever a side to be lightly regarded, but because at home in the first leg we had gained a splendid 4-1 victory and we had therefore travelled to Madrid with a three goals advantage. Yet we lost 1-5.

And now to this year's editorial and more

Charlie George (left) and Leighton James (right) welcome the 'new boy', Derek Hales, to Derby County's striking force.

than ever before I am wondering about how different the end of season picture will be from how it seems now early in January 1977.

I suppose it is the events of the first half of the 1976–77 season at the Baseball Ground that have brought home to me just how constantly, and often unexpectedly, changes are made in football. At Derby there had been a difficult period late in 1973 after the departure of Brian Clough and the arrival of the club's old skipper, Dave Mackay, as manager. But, as I have already mentioned, by 1975 we were back on the top as the League Champions and we had ended the 1975–76 season in a respectable fourth place.

With the relatively short time—compared with other careers—that any player can expect to command a regular first team place in first class football, and understanding that it is a vital part of any manager's job to be looking ahead and grooming replacement players, it is fairly commonplace to see new faces in the

line-up of even the top sides when new seasons get off to their usual hectic start. Not many people were surprised I suppose when Francis Lee decided to hang up his boots. After all so far as Franny was concerned, Manchester City had apparently decided that his First Division days were over when they let him come to Derby—where he turned in so many fine displays.

But if his absence from Derby's team for the 1976–77 season was no great surprise, who would have foretold that before the end of 1976, Dave Mackay the manager would have departed? Or after Mr Mackay had gone, that Bruce Rioch would have been transferred to Everton? Or that the prolific scorer for Charlton Athletic, Derek Hales, would have come to Derby to tackle First Division defences for the first time?

But that is what has happened. You—and I—will know better by the time you are reading this annual after the end of the 1976–77 season, how Derby as a whole have fared under "new management"; how Derek Hales has been able to cope in the First Division. Has he retained his scoring flair? Or has his presence in Derby's attack given more chances to players like Leighton James to pop in the goals? For that matter, leaving my personal interest in Derby's progress aside, how has Bruce Rioch fitted into things at Goodison Park? And not only Bruce Rioch—what of Duncan McKenzie?

At the start of the season Duncan had gone off to the famous Belgium club, Anderlecht. With his skilful, individualistic style of play most people would have expected him to settle quickly into the Anderlecht team. Indeed it seems that the Anderlecht fans immediately accepted him and warmed to his play. Yet— and a change of manager and of tactics at Anderlecht played a part in this—Duncan's first team place was never certain with the Belgian club and Everton stepped in and brought him back into English football.

I have paused a while, with the thought of the unexpected happenings in mind, and glanced back through the past five ALL STARS annuals and re-read some of the contributions. A sort of check on what has happened to some of what I might call the ALL STARS "Old Boys".

In the 1973 annual, the first I edited, the previous editor Jim Armfield was a contributor. Amongst other pertinent comments Jim Armfield wrote that "Fans, I now realise, criticise managers more than they do players". There have been several instances of players who have been more or less driven away from clubs because the fans, or at least a noisy section of them, have made them the target for constant barracking. But I expect Jim Armfield was right that it is the manager who is likely to get most of the brickbats shied at him when a team is not doing well.

Jim Armfield was then, of course, manager of Bolton. Since then he has moved to Leeds and has the job of re-building the first team of that famous club. What a change there has been at Elland Road with the departure of players like Billy Bremner, Norman Hunter and Terry Yorath (the latter one of the victims of barracking by the home fans).

There was a Leeds player contributing to that 1973 annual—Terry Cooper—and he too, after his career as an England player had been prematurely ended by injuries, soon left Leeds to rejoin his old team-mate Jack Charlton at Middlesbrough. Two other 1973 contributors have been the victims of injuries—Colin Bell, so sorely missed by Manchester City and by England for a twelve-month and still, as I write now, not certain of ever resuming his career; and Tony Green who, soon after he had moved from Blackpool to Newcastle, did have to permanently hang up his boots. Of the rest of the 1973 contributors, Steve Heighway and Ray Clemence are still with Liverpool, and Alex Stepney with Manchester United but Rodney Marsh, then with Manchester City, has moved elsewhere.

There has been a game of musical chairs amongst three of the 1974 contributors—Joe Royle, Rodney Marsh again, and Bob Latchford. Then they were with Everton, Manchester City and Birmingham respectively. Now it is Bob Latchford who is at Everton, Joe Royle at Manchester City, whilst Rodney Marsh has returned to Craven Cottage where his first class career began with Fulham.

There were two happy contributions in the 1974 annual. Ian Callaghan revealed that "in the first week of September 1972, I played in a Second Round Football League Cup-tie at Carlisle—and went into the record books. For

The shot from Bobby Stokes of Southampton that meant a Cup runners-up, and not a winners, medal for Alex Stepney in the 1976 F.A. Cup Final

that game was my 533rd for Liverpool, and at the end of it, I had overtaken the club record of 532 matches which had been set—and held for years—by the great Billy Liddell." Ian ended his article—"I hope I can keep going for a few more seasons and chalk up some more games".

Well, those few more seasons have come and gone; Liverpool have remained a top flight club and, whilst others have come and gone, Ian Callaghan has carried on.

The other particularly happy story—with our advantage of knowing what the seasons since 1973 have brought—was Mike Channon's with his admission that "obviously I hope to stay at the top for as long as possible. It would be nice to win more caps and perhaps pick up a Cup or League medal."

Since then Mike Channon's club, Southampton, have dropped out of the First Division and there was considerable speculation about whether Mike would stay with a Second Division club and, if he did, whether that would lose him his England place. He has stayed; he has not lost his England place and, a just reward, he has picked up a Cup winner's medal.

Mention of Mike Channon's medal—gained when Southampton beat Manchester United 1-0 in the 1976 F.A. Cup Final, reminds me of Alex Stepney's contribution in last year's annual. When he wrote his piece Alex, as he mentioned, had lost his place in Manchester United's side when Tommy Docherty announced he was going to give Paddy Roche his chance. I suppose Tommy Docherty's thinking was that Alex had had a long run since moving from the then amateur club Tooting and Mitcham to Millwall in 1963 and that it was the manager's job to find a suitable replacement. In fact—as is the way of many keepers (Peter Bonetti with Chelsea is another recent example)—Alex was soon back between the sticks for United and many argued that had he not missed those few vital matches Manchester United might have won the 1975–76 Championship instead of finishing third just four points behind Liverpool the winners.

What reminded me of Alex's article however was his stated ambition that he wanted to make a hat-trick of Wembley games. First, as he wrote, he had played there for England against Sweden; then, the second time, for Manchester United when they beat Benfica in the European Champions Cup Final. But—Alex went on—"my ambition, before I finally hang up my goalkeeper's gloves, is to make it a hat-trick—by playing in an F.A. Cup Final and collecting a winner's medal."

Well, half of that ambition was fulfilled—although who would have thought that at the time that Alex Stepney wrote his piece. He did play in the 1976 F.A. Cup Final but it was Mike Channon's Saints who went up to collect the winners' medals. Alex had to be content with one for the runners-up.

I see that I jumped from Mike Channon writing for the 1974 annual to Alex Stepney writing for the 1977 one, and I have little space left for dwelling much longer on the annuals between. But everywhere there are examples of the ups and downs, the changes—some asked for by the players, some more or less forced upon them—that make a professional footballer's career such a hazardous one. There are the bright sides and the bleak ones. In the 1975 annual two Queens Park Rangers wrote—soon after Rangers had made the First Division. To date the football gods have smiled kindly on Phil Parkes and Dave Thomas. Both have gained England caps. Both have shared in many great wins for the London club—still, as I write, carrying England's flag in the 1976–77 UEFA Cup competition after particularly fine victories over Slovan Bratislava (with more than half the Czechoslovakian side) and Cologne.

There is a contrast in the fortunes of two big Scottish lads who contributed to the 1975 annual—Gordon McQueen and Jim Holton. At that time Gordon, settled in the Leeds side, was wondering if he would get a chance in Scotland's team. Jim was, it seemed, well established in Manchester United's and Scotland's teams. Both have since suffered badly from time lost through injuries but now, whilst Jim Holton's career has slipped back, Gordon McQueen has, after about a season's absence, returned to both the Leeds and Scotland teams.

Finally I must mention two of the 1976 contributors—the brothers Brian and Jimmy Greenhoff. Younger brother Brian wrote of his high regard for Jimmy as a striker and how he was looking forward to playing for Manchester United against Stoke City with Jimmy playing for them. Brian then, as he wrote at the beginning of his article, was a comparative newcomer to United's squad but he has progressed rapidly and already collected England caps. But I suspect one of the happiest days for Brian Greenhoff—and for Jimmy—was when late in 1976 they learned that Jimmy was on his way from Stoke to join his younger brother at Old Trafford.

GOALS ARE MY BUSINESS

JOHN TOSHACK

Goals are my business—and by the end of last season, I had scored close on 200, which meant that I had averaged a goal in something just over every other game. And you can take it from me that all goals are good ones . . . because they are always hard to get.

Of course, there is the odd goal that comes your way and can be regarded as a "gift". But a striker never needs to look a gift horse in the mouth, because there are many times when you know you have hit a shot or sent in a header which is well worth a goal—only to see the 'keeper make a spectacular save. Or a lucky one. And the thing is that, in the final analysis, every goal counts.

I mentioned the odd lucky goal. Well, I think there is no doubt about the one which was the fluke of all time, so far as I'm concerned. It came in a game against Queen's Park Rangers, when the ball was crossed from the right wing, and I went to meet it. I swung my right foot at the ball—and missed. The ball hit my left leg . . . and trickled over the line, with 'keeper Phil Parkes beaten to the wide. He had anticipated my catching the ball with my right foot, and dived that way; when the ball hit my left leg, he was stranded.

But if that goal was a bit of good luck for me, I paid the price, because when I swung so hard with my right leg, and missed, I pulled a hamstring, and I took no further part in the game.

Hat-tricks?—I've scored five altogether in my career, and one of them was against Queen's Park Rangers, too,

Liverpool's famous scoring tandem of Kevin Keegan (he's the one on top!) and John Toshack—pictured here after Liverpool had won the UEFA Cup against Bruges in May 1976

A happy picture of three Liverpool defenders selected for England's World Cup squad to play Italy in November 1976. From left to right: Phil Thompson, skipper Emlyn Hughes and Ray Clemence.

in my days with Cardiff City. I also scored a hat-trick for Cardiff against Hull City, shortly before I was transferred to Liverpool. In fact, I seem to remember that Liverpool were watching me, that day.

The other hat-tricks have come during my career at Liverpool—one against Birmingham at Anfield, one against West Ham at Upton Park, and one against Hibernian in the U.E.F.A. Cup at Anfield. And that last one was probably the most vital one of all.

We had gone to Hibs for the first leg of the U.E.F.A. Cup-tie, and returned home a goal down. So we knew we had to score a couple in the second leg at Anfield. As it turned out,

we needed to score three, for Hibs got a goal in the second game, and if the match had finished level at 2-2, on aggregate, they would have gone through to the next round on the rule that away goals count double. My third goal made sure that it was Liverpool who went through . . . and we finished up by winning the U.E.F.A. Cup, as well as the League championship, in season 1975–76.

Being a Welshman, I'm naturally extremely proud of having been chosen to play for Wales, and on the international scene, I must admit that my first goal for my country still remains one of my proudest moments in top-class football. The game was against Scot-

land, at Wrexham, and I was still a Cardiff player. The goalkeeper I beat was Tommy Lawrence . . . who was also Liverpool's 'keeper. So later we were to become club-mates.

Apart from being my first goal for Wales, it was one on which I can look back with every satisfaction, because it really was a good 'un. I collected the ball about 25 yards out, and hit it on the volley—and you don't get many of those.

With Liverpool, I've had some exciting moments and played in some great games. When you collect winner's medals in the League, in Europe and the F.A. Cup, you know you're really achieving something. And one of the most priceless goals I scored came in season 1975–76, when we travelled to play Barcelona in the semi-finals of the U.E.F.A. Cup.

Remember, I had scored a hat-trick against Hibs in an earlier round, to keep us on the European trail . . . Well, when we went to Barcelona, who had Johan Cruyff and Neeskens in their side, we knew we had a much tougher proposition on our hands. Barcelona had been beaten on their own ground in European competition only by Real Madrid, and they were confidently being tipped to come to Anfield for the return game with some sort of a lead.

In fact, it was Liverpool who provided the shocks for the home supporters, and John Toshack who produced the pay-off punch which really had Barcelona sagging at the knees. Goalkeeper Ray Clemence sent a long clearance upfield, and Kevin Keegan and I moved in to link together. I played the ball to Kevin, he returned the compliment—and I stuck the ball past the Barcelona 'keeper.

That was a night which I shall never forget, for we really did stun the opposition and their supporters. At the end of the match, the disappointed home fans rained cushions down on to the pitch, to show how they felt about this unexpected defeat of their idols. And when Barcelona came to Anfield, Phil Thompson got the goal which ensured we went into the final, even though Barcelona scored themselves.

I mentioned that Kevin Keegan and I linked up in the move which brought me that winning goal in Barcelona, and I think it's a good time now to tell you about my partnership with Kevin. Some people seemed to take a long time to realise that we had something special going for us, and when the penny dropped, they felt they had made a sudden discovery. "It's telepathic, that understanding between them," they said.

Telepathic or not, Kevin and I had been working well together in our Soccer "double act" quite a long time before people began to take notice. In fact, the first time we played together was in a pre-season practice match, shortly after Kevin had arrived at Anfield . . . and we scored three or four goals between us.

Then, when Kevin made his debut at Anfield in front of the Kop, I laid on a goal for him. In season 1972–73, when Liverpool played Borussia Moenchengladbach in the first leg of the U.E.F.A. Cup final at Anfield, we were at it again—and two of our three goals were claimed by Kevin. And so, for quite a few seasons, we really developed our partnership—even if it seemed to take people a while before they caught on.

Usually, it does take time for a striker to settle in up front with a new partner. But somehow, it seemed that Kevin and myself never had this sort of problem. Right from the start, we hit it off and made goals for each other, and while there obviously was a contrast in styles between us, the pattern as a whole was just what the doctor ordered. He buzzed around, going out wide sometimes, but so often the pair of us were only a few yards apart, in the 18-yard box, and then we would turn on the "double act".

When you look at Liverpool as a whole, and examine their record through the past dozen years or so, the one thing which stands out is that they have been consistent. The names and faces may have changed, but the style has been the same—and so has the run of success.

Consistency is what brings results and trophies, and Liverpool have maintained consistency, right the way through. The same thing applies to strikers—you've got to be consistently sticking the ball away, if you're to become recognised as a danger-man in the goalmouth area. And in all modesty, I think I can claim to have maintained the sort of consistency which makes defenders respect a striker.

In 161 League games for Cardiff, I totalled 74 goals; in 19 European matches for Cardiff, I hit 11 goals. And I have carried on the scoring during my seasons with Liverpool. For instance, I had scored 70 goals in just over 150 League appearances; and in fewer than 250 games for Liverpool altogether, I was getting close to the century mark for goals. Which meant that in something over 400 matches during my career, I was heading for a double century of goals.

As I said at the start, goals are my business, and sometimes you have to go in where it hurts, to get them. You get the odd lucky goal, you hit the near-perfect goal now and again . . . but when you look back, and add up all the times the ball went into the opposition's net, you say to yourself: "Yes, every goal was a good 'un." And I like to think that, right through my career with Cardiff, Liverpool and Wales, I've done my job as it should be done—tucking away the chances. And the record book shows that I've succeeded.

Would You Believe It?
Stan Liversedge

Second Division Southampton on their triumphant tour of the city after winning the 1976 F.A. Cup Final against the firm favourites Manchester United. Unmistakably Mike Channon, holding the Cup, with Peter Osgood (left) and manager, Lawrie McMenemy, beside him.

Eleven years have gone by, since England won the World Cup; and next year, it's another World Cup competition in Argentina. England have had varying fortunes between the two World Cup competitions, and so have some of the top clubs in the country. Who, for instance, would have imagined Manchester United playing in the Second Division, if only for a season? And who would have tipped Second Division Sunderland to beat First Division Leeds, and Southampton to beat Manchester United, in F.A. Cup Finals at Wembley?

I doubt if you would have forecast, either, that George Best, Rodney Marsh and Bobby Moore would team up together at Fulham; that Don Revie would have been tempted to leave Leeds and take up the England team-manager's job; or that Bill Shankly would ever have laid down the reins as manager of Liverpool.

If you had asked a virtually unknown amateur player in 1970 what the future held for him, he would probably have said that when he completed his studies at university and obtained his degree, he would go into teaching. Almost

17

The Man Who Came Back—1. Duncan McKenzie (centre) in action for Everton against Coventry after his return from a brief sojourn with the Belgian club, Anderlecht.

certainly he would never have prophesied that in the next seven years he would be winning medals in the First Division, the F.A. Cup and in Europe.

Yet this happened to Steve Heighway, who had made a name for himself playing with Skelmersdale United, in the Cheshire League. He was signed by Liverpool, pitched into their League side in a matter of months, and went to Wembley in his first full season, went there again in 1974, and in 1973 and 1976 collected medals for the First Division championship and the U.E.F.A. Cup.

Would Kevin Keegan ever have dared to dream, when he was playing for Scunthorpe, that one day he would be valued at around a million pounds, with clubs such as Real Madrid, Barcelona and Juventus all eager to sign him?—Kevin, so the story goes, might not even have become a Liverpool player, if Preston had had the money to buy him from Scunthorpe . . .

Alan Ball was the manager of North End then, and the tale goes that he tried to sign Keegan for Preston. The offer was £25,000— and Scunthorpe wanted £10,000 more than that figure. But Preston couldn't afford the extra cash, and Liverpool came along and got Keegan for £35,000. It was Andy Beattie, who had managed several clubs in England, as well as the Scotland international side, who recommended Kevin to Liverpool—just as he had recommended the youngster to other clubs. Liverpool didn't know it then, but they were getting the bargain of the century.

Then there was Stan Bowles. He had been at Manchester City and Bury, and that appeared to be the end of a League career for him, promising though his talent seemed to be. Along came Crewe Alexandra, to give him another chance, and he made sufficient of an impression that Carlisle were persuaded to pay Crewe around £12,000 for him. When Carlisle sold Stan to Queen's Park Rangers, they got

£100,000 . . . and his value as an England international has soared since then.

It is doubtful if we would have forecast that players from English League clubs would sign for clubs on the Continent—Duncan McKenzie, Peter Anderson, Martin Chivers, Roger Davies, Terry Lees . . . they all went abroad. Lees' career took a turn he probably never expected, for he had had a spell with his home-town club, Stoke City, been to Crewe on loan, and moved to Port Vale in exchange for a £3,000 transfer fee—then Rotterdam Sparta paid Vale 10 times that amount.

Would you have tipped Brian Clough to take Derby County to the League championship, and have brief encounters with Brighton and Leeds United, before settling down to the job of turning Nottingham Forest into a promotion-chasing side? Or expected Bobby Charlton and Jack Charlton to become rival managers, for a spell?

Terry Paine played hundreds of games for Southampton, and most people, surely, would have expected him to remain with the Saints until his final League game. But he went to Hereford, finally decided that it was time to quit—and was called out of retirement to help them when they were struggling. By that time, he had played 800 matches . . . and Ian Callag-han was almost on the same mark, too, with his one and only club, Liverpool.

Yet only a few years ago, it seemed that "Cally", like several others of the great Liverpool side of the 1960's, would soon be preparing to bow out, for after a cartilage operation, he had a real battle to regain not only fitness, but form. Yet he persevered, and reclaimed a First Division place, to carry on collecting honours, including the Footballer of the Year award.

It is doubtful if you would have expected to see Soccer taking root in the U.S., and some of our established players going out there to play during the summer months, thus making their careers an all-the-year-round occupation.

Would you have tipped Malcolm Allison to be acting as Soccer consultant to Galatasaray, a team in Turkey, with the route having led from Maine-road via Crystal Palace? Or Jimmy Hill selling Soccer expertise to the Saudi Arabians, with manager Bill McGarry, once of Ipswich and Wolves, the man at the helm of this crusade?

Would you have guessed that, after the feats of Glasgow Celtic in 1967 and Manchester United in 1968, no other British club would have won the European Cup in the next decade; or that clubs such as Liverpool,

A youthful Franz Beckenbauer (white shirt) in action for West Germany against Switzerland in the 1966 World Cup Final Tournament in England

The Man Who Came Back — 2. George Best, back in English football, and pictured playing for Fulham against Wolves.

Leeds, Arsenal and Newcastle would have made such an impact in the U.E.F.A. Cup?

Think of the names in the England team which won the 1966 World Cup: Banks; Cohen, Wilson; Stiles, Jack Charlton, Moore; Ball, Hunt, Bobby Charlton, Hurst, Peters.

You would never have forecast that Gordon Banks would have his career cut short by a car accident; that Nobby Stiles would become the right-hand man of first Bobby Charlton, then Harry Catterick, at Preston; that Geoff Hurst would leave West Ham for Stoke, and finish up as the team boss of non-leaguers Telford; that Alan Ball would move from Blackpool to Everton to Arsenal to Southampton; or that Martin Peters would play for West Ham and Spurs, and for Norwich.

Would you have guessed, also, that Franz Beckenbauer, who was a mere 21-year-old in that losing West German World Cup-final side of 1966, would be leading his country 10 years later as they gained revenge more than once on England? And there was a youngster who played for Ajax when they stuck five goals past Liverpool . . . little did you realise that Johan Cruyff would become a superstar in Europe.

All these things came to pass in football, during the 10 years and more which have gone by since England won the World Cup. And when you stop to think about it, it makes you wonder what the next 10 years in Soccer will bring. Or even the next 12 months.

During the past decade, Liverpool and Leeds have had the lion's share of the headlines and the honours, as they have powered their way through matches at home and abroad. The Leeds machine began to stutter, while Liverpool carried on; and new challengers arose, such as Ipswich Town, under Bobby Robson's managership, and Manchester City, with Tony Book at the helm.

Gordon Lee was another manager who before moving to Everton hit the headlines at Newcastle—controversial headlines, too, as it became plain that the Newcastle fans' scoring hero, Malcolm Macdonald, might be allowed to leave St. James's Park. Surely one never imagined that "Supermac" would ever be allowed to go; yet after he went, and the tears had subsided and the dust had settled, Newcastle fought their way into a challenging position for the championship.

So even in the last 12 months or so, events have moved quickly in Soccer; and things will undoubtedly happen in the next year, too. Football, the man said, is a funny game. How else could Matlock go and win 5-2 in the F.A. Cup at Mansfield, or Northwich Victoria dispose of League opposition such as Rochdale, Peterborough and Watford?

Yes, Soccer has seen some changes which we would never have dared to forecast, and there will be more to come. Some people have forecast that the game will destroy itself, before very much longer; but no matter what perils may lie ahead for clubs and individuals, the one safe bet is that the game will not die. Because too many people are involved.

The ALL STARS QUIZ
BY J.M. JEFFERY

Round and About . . .

1. In which city would you find Hearts and Hibernians playing at home?

2. Liverpool F.C. obviously come from Liverpool in Lancashire, while Tranmere Rovers are at home in Birkenhead just across the River Mersey. But which other League club comes from Liverpool?

3. Wales play most of their home games at Ninian Park, the home of Cardiff City, but they also use the ground of another Football League club. Which club?

Let's travel abroad . . .

4. In which two important Dutch cities would you find the Ajax and Feyenoord clubs?

5. Can you name the two Italian First Division clubs who play their home games at the San Siro Stadium?

6. Perhaps the most famous club side in the World over the past two decades has been Santos F.C. Which country boasts Santos as one of their leading clubs?

7. A top-ranking Spanish club has won the European Champion Clubs Cup more times than any other. Which club?

8. Another club with a fine European Cup record is Benfica . . . from which country?

9. Which successful West German club won the European Cup while captained by Franz Beckenbauer, who also led the German national side to victory in the '74 World Cup?

10. With which Middle East country is Jimmy Hill connected?

The European Championship '76 . . .

11. Who won the European Championship in 1976?

12. In which country were the semi-finals and final held?

13. The success of the winning side was not without significance for English fans. Why?

14. Can you name the sole British national side to qualify for the quarter-finals?

Famous Names . . .

15. In the 1960's quite a few British players went abroad to play for foreign sides, among them Denis Law, Gerry Hitchens, and Jimmy Greaves. In 1976 a Leeds United player was transferred to a Belgian side for several months before being signed by Everton. Which player?

16. Let's try a few nick-names. Who are . . . The Gunners; Pompey; The Rams; The Posh; The Hammers; The Bees?

17. Watford's chairman is a personality outside of football. Do you know who he is?

18. Eric Morecambe, better known as half of the Morecambe and Wise duo, seems prone to shouting "Arsenal" when on television. But which other League club has held his interest?

Round the Grounds . . .

19. Which of the following grounds were the homes of First Division clubs in the 1976–77 season . . . Elland Road; St. Andrew's; The Valley; Goldstone Ground; Hillsborough; Ayresome Park; Filbert Street?

20. Can you name all seven clubs whose grounds are listed in the previous question?

21. There are two League clubs in Bristol. City play at Ashton Gate, but what about Rovers?

22. Loftus Road is the homely ground of Queens Park Rangers. Some years ago however, Rangers tried an experiment by playing some home games at a larger, nearby stadium, an historic athletics arena. Which stadium?

23. Due to intensive bomb damage to their Old Trafford ground during the last War, a leading English club were forced to play their home games at the nearby Maine Road ground, home of another leading club. Can you name both clubs?

24. Hampden Park is home for Scotland's national side, but which Scottish League club plays at home there?

With the NASL . . . *I hope you've read the relevant article!*

25. What do the initials NASL stand for?

26. When was the NASL founded?

27. In 1967 the National Professional Soccer League recruited domestic and foreign talent to build its teams, rather like the NASL does at present. However, the rival US Association imported entire foreign sides. Washington Whips, represented by Scotland's Aberdeen lost the final 6-5 in extra-time to Los Angeles Wolves, represented by England's . . . Guess Who? The answer's in the nickname.

28. What is the connection between Los Angeles Aztecs and Fulham?

29. Which NASL team boasts Pelé's talents?

The F.A. Cup . . .

30. Second Division Southampton surprised the football world when they beat Manchester United 1-0 in the 1976 Cup Final. Who scored the vital goal late in the second half?

31. Southampton were the third Second Division side to reach the Final, and the second to

On the plane bringing the England party back from Helsin

win the Cup, in the four seasons from 1973 until 1976. Can you name the other two Second Division finalists?

32. When was the first F.A. Cup competition held?

With the Schoolboys . . .

33. The English Schools F.A. Inter-Association Trophy is the schoolboys' equivalent of the F.A. Cup, with over 200 District teams competing at under 15 years level. Season 1975–76 saw Slough Schools F.A. lose 4-3 on aggregate

...ad had beaten Finland 4-1 in their opening match in their World Cup Qualifying Group. Playing backgammon are Mike Channon and . . . . . ? (see Question 17)

in the Final, winning 1-0 at home but losing 2-4 at Anfield. Who were the winning Association, recording their twelfth championship?

34. The Victory Shield is played for each season by the Schoolboy International sides of the four home countries, England, Northern Ireland, Scotland, and Wales. In 1974–75 England finished top with 6 points, Wales second with 4 points, Ireland third with 2 points, and Scotland surprisingly bottom after being beaten in all three games. Who won the Victory Shield the following season, in 1976?

35. The Southern Counties Evening Post Shield is a knockout competition for Primary School (under 11) District teams covering an area from Portsmouth, to Bath, to Luton, to Aldershot. Season 1975–76 saw Oxford City Primary Schools win the two-leg Final, beating the schoolboys from the South Coast port whose professional side went one better at Wembley. Which port?

Answers on page 61

The Story of the Under-23 Internationals

by COLIN TODD

On March 23rd 1976 England played what seems almost certain to be their last Under-23 International match and so ended a chapter in our football history that had begun on January 20th 1954—before, that is to say, most of the players who proudly wore the England shirt in that last match had been born!

The date of England's first Under-23 match is a significant one—it was two months after the Full national team had suffered their first defeat at home against foreign opposition when the famous Hungarian side of players

A flash-back to 1969 and a picture taken of the England U-23 squad in training before the international against the Soviet Union to be played at Old Trafford. For the record England won 2-0. How many of these players can you recognise before reading on? How many later won Full International caps?
(Standing—left to right) John Hurst, Emlyn Hughes, Sam Ellis, Joe Corrigan, David Nish, Colin Todd, David Parkin, (Front row—left to right) Brian Kidd, Joe Royle, Peter Osgood, Jimmy Husband, John Aston and Alun Evans. Seven won Full caps—Hughes, Corrigan, Nish, Todd, Kidd, Royle and Osgood.

Steve Coppell, seen (right) in action for Manchester United against Coventry's Terry Yorath, played in England's last Under-23 International

like Puskas, Bozsik, Hidegkuti and Kocsis came to Wembley and won by six goals to three. Then began the 'inquest' into the state of English football and the International Selection Committee introduced their policy of developing young players by means of "B" and "Under-23" matches—a policy put more quickly into practice of course when that Wembley defeat was followed only six months later by an even more humiliating one in Budapest where the Hungarians won 7-1.

Yet the very first Under-23 international, played as it was between those two Hungarian victories over England, did not get much publicity even in the Football Association's own Year Book. That showed the score—Italy "Under-23" 3 England "Under-23" 0—but made no mention of the match nor included any report or line-ups.

For the record however here is the England Under-23 team that played that January afternoon in Bologna: Wood (Manchester United):

Gunter (Portsmouth), Ellis (Charlton); White-foot (Manchester United), Dodgin (Arsenal), Edwards (Manchester United); Finney (Sheffield Wednesday), Broadbent (Wolves), Leary (Charlton), Nicholls (West Bromwich Albion) and Blunstone (Chelsea).

The description "Under-23" had not caught on at the time and in some of the annuals and magazines of that time you will find the match listed as being played between Young Italy and Young England. That description could have been confusing because, since 1948, England had pioneered the Youth International Tournament that has been so successful. There was however the gap between playing for England in Youth International matches—and by so doing getting the *feeling* for international football; getting used to meeting team-mates for perhaps the first time and learning as quickly as possible how to combine with them on the field of play; and, this too is important, how to get on with them off the field of play so that a good club atmosphere soon develops. There was this long gap before the promising Youth player was ready for the Full national side. So the policy of the Under-23 and the B international matches.

Somehow the "B" matches never became so

England's Kevin Keegan and Wales' Terry Yorath tussle for possession in the British Home Championship match played in May 1976. Both were former Under-23 Internationals.

ENGLAND'S UNDER-23 INTERNATIONAL RECORD—1954–1976

Opponents	Home						Away						Total					
	P	W	D	L	F	A	P	W	D	L	F	A	P	W	D	L	F	A
Austria	1	1	0	0	3	0	1	0	1	0	0	0	2	1	1	0	3	0
Belgium	1	1	0	0	6	1	1	1	0	0	1	0	2	2	0	0	7	1
Bulgaria	2	2	0	0	10	3	2	0	1	1	2	3	4	2	1	1	12	6
Czechoslovakia	4	3	1	0	7	1	4	1	2	1	3	4	8	4	3	1	10	5
Denmark	2	1	1	0	6	2	2	1	1	0	4	1	4	2	2	0	10	3
France	3	2	1	0	5	0	3	0	3	0	5	5	6	2	4	0	10	5
E. Germany	1	0	0	1	0	1	2	1	1	0	6	3	3	1	1	1	6	4
W. Germany	3	3	0	0	11	3	3	1	1	1	3	3	6	4	1	1	14	6
Greece	1	1	0	0	5	0	1	0	1	0	0	0	2	1	1	0	5	0
Hungary	3	2	0	1	7	2	3	0	0	3	1	6	6	2	0	4	8	8
Israel	1	1	0	0	7	1	2	1	0	1	4	4	3	2	0	1	11	5
Italy	3	2	1	0	7	2	3	1	1	1	4	4	6	3	2	1	11	6
Netherlands	3	2	1	0	10	5	3	1	0	2	6	5	6	3	1	2	16	10
Poland	2	1	1	0	4	1	2	2	0	0	6	2	4	3	1	0	10	3
Portugal	2	2	0	0	6	0	2	1	1	0	4	3	4	3	1	0	10	3
Rumania	2	2	0	0	8	2	2	1	0	1	1	1	4	3	0	1	9	3
Scotland	7	4	1	2	14	10	9	5	4	0	24	11	16	9	5	2	38	21
Sweden	1	1	0	0	2	0	—	—	—	—	—	—	1	1	0	0	2	0
Switzerland	1	0	1	0	1	1	—	—	—	—	—	—	1	0	1	0	1	1
Turkey	2	2	0	0	6	1	2	1	0	1	3	3	4	3	0	1	9	4
U.S.S.R.	1	1	0	0	2	0	1	0	1	0	0	0	2	1	1	0	2	0
Wales	6	4	2	0	15	1	7	5	1	1	14	6	13	9	3	1	29	7
Yugoslavia	2	1	1	0	2	1	2	1	0	1	4	3	4	2	1	1	6	4

In addition the England U-23 team was twice engaged in matches that were abandoned. Once against Scotland when England were leading 3-1 and once against Turkey before either side had scored.

The full record for the completed matches is:—

P	W	D	L	F	A
111	63	30	18	239	105

popular with the British associations as they have been with continental countries where it was a regular practice to arrange fixtures with two national "A" teams, "B" teams and, later, the Under-23 teams meeting each other on the same or on consecutive days.

But if England dropped out of playing "B" international matches after some five or six seasons, the Under-23 matches have become very useful until, as you can see from the table that accompanies this article, no less than 111 matches were played—113 if you like to include a couple that had to be abandoned!

The first one, as I have mentioned, was against Italy in Bologna in January 1954 and we lost 0-3. That was the only Under-23 match played in 1954 but there were three matches played in 1955—and in the first of these at Stamford Bridge England had their revenge over Italy when they won 5-1 in January. A few weeks later the first England-Scotland

Under-23 match was played in Glasgow and England won 6-0.

Soon after the 1955–56 season began England entertained Denmark's Under-23 team at Portsmouth and on September 28, chalked up another 5-1 victory. The F.A. Year Book was now taking notice of the Under-23 matches and reported that "an even first-half was followed by a brilliant display by Haynes." Yes, that was of course Johnny Haynes, later to become England's captain and to make 56 appearances for the Full England team. The line-up against Denmark was:

Matthews (Coventry); P. Sillett (Chelsea), G. Shaw (Sheffield United); Anderson (Sunderland), T. Smith (Birmingham), Clayton (Blackburn Rovers); Kaye (Barnsley), Robson (Fulham), Stokes (Tottenham), Haynes (Fulham), Blunstone (Chelsea).

Robson (Fulham) is now the very successful manager of Ipswich Town. He, like Matthews,

Sillett, Shaw, Anderson, Smith, Clayton, Haynes and Blunstone went on to win Full international caps. All that team in fact except Kaye and Stokes graduated from the Under-23s to the Full International team. And that does seem to indicate how right was the policy adopted by the International Selection Committee back in the early fifties. The full facts are that between 1954 and 1976, 297 players appeared for England in Under-23 matches and 137 of them had won Full International caps by the end of the 1975–76 season.

For many of those 137 the gradual progress to the Full national team had begun with schoolboy and then youth international matches, with the Under-23s the last rung of the ladder before that Full international appearance.

It was natural that UEFA would take an interest in Under-23 international matches as they became a regular feature of the European football scene and since 1970 UEFA have organised a European Challenge Cup competition for national Under-23 teams. The competition that spreads over two seasons runs parallel with the European Football Championship and World Cup qualifying competition for the Full national teams and, as far as has been possible, with teams competing in the same qualifying groups for each competition.

So far the competition has been rather monopolised by the Soviet bloc countries with the first two-legged Final for the 1970–72 competition between Czechoslovakia and the Soviet Union. Czechoslovakia won with a 3-1 win in Ostrava after drawing two-all in Moscow. Hungary and East Germany were the 1972–74 finalists. Each won their home leg but Hungary's 4-0, compared with East Germany's 3-2, gave them the Cup. Then the last competition (1974–76) was between the Soviet Union and Hungary. A one-all draw in Budapest and a 2-1 win in Moscow brought victory for the Soviet Union.

England did not enter the first two competitions but came in for the last one and, compensating a bit for the failure of the national team in a similar group for the European Football Championship (that is the old Nations Cup), easily headed Portugal and Czechoslovakia, for a place in the quarter-final. Then England were drawn against Hungary—and that brings me back to the record of the Under-23's as a whole.

Just take a look at the table. I think you will agree that England's record is a pretty good one

with only one opponent having the edge over us —but that one is Hungary. Nor need we be surprised that it was the Hungarians who, in 1959, were the first to win an Under-23 match in England. Since then Scotland twice and East Germany have also won on English soil but against those four home defeats (out of 54 matches played) we can boast of away victories against Belgium, Czechoslovakia, Denmark, both East and West Germany, Israel, Italy, the Netherlands, Poland, Portugal, Rumania, Turkey, Yugoslavia and, of course, Scotland and Wales. But in all three visits to Hungary we were beaten. The last time was in March 1976 when we lost 0-3. A fortnight later we played the second leg of the quarter-final at Manchester. The Hungarians scored first which meant that, with away goals counting double if the aggregated scores of the two legs were level, England needed to win 5-1. It was too much despite a fine display and the following team had to be content with a 3-1 win: Wallington (Leicester); Nattrass and Kennedy (both Newcastle); Brian Greenhoff (Manchester United), Lock (West Ham), Wilkins (Chelsea); Coppell (Manchester United), Case (Liverpool), Pearson (Manchester United), Paddon (then West Ham), and Hill (Manchester United).

Before that match was played and the 1974–76 UEFA Under-23 competition moved on to its completion in June, the future of Under-23 matches was being discussed. Players all over Europe seem to make the leap from Youth to Full internationals at an ever younger age and at a Conference of the Presidents and General Secretaries of the member Football Associations of UEFA there was overwhelming support for replacing the Under-23 competition with one for Under-21 representative national teams. The Executive Committee of UEFA supported the idea and 24 national associations, including England and Scotland, have entered for the first competition (1976–78). The Under-21 age limit is not completely binding. Each team will be allowed two players not subject to it but the rest of the team will be players born on or after August 1st 1955.

England, at the time of writing, have played one friendly Under-21 match against Wales with the result a somewhat disappointing goalless draw but later we should qualify in a group made up with Finland and Norway. What will be interesting over the next few seasons is noting how quickly Under-21 players make the jump to the Full national side.

Ray Clemence in goal for England against Wales

Colin Todd

Brian Greenhoff

John Toshack

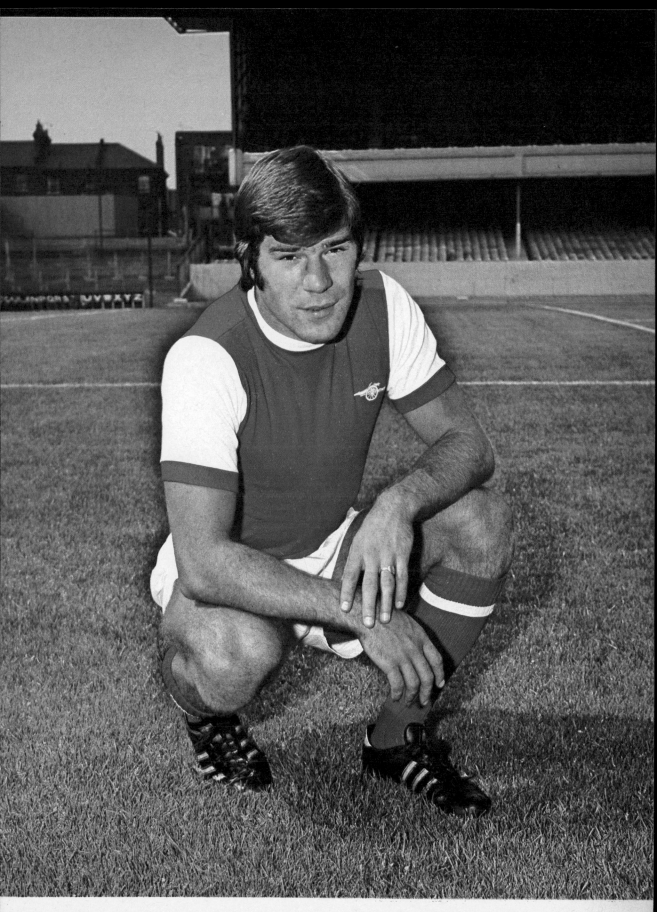

Malcolm Macdonald

Mick Mills

34

Joe Royle

Kevin Keegan

You've been FAN-tastic!

Lou Macari

Lou Macari and Sammy McIlroy salute another United goal.

Manchester United could turn out half a team for England, half a team for Ireland, and half a team for Scotland—well, near enough, anyway. Yes, Old Trafford is the scene for a regular gathering of the clans, not to mention the fans, on match days.

England?—Goalkeeper Alex Stepney, centre-half Brian Greenhoff, and forwards Gordon Hill, Stuart Pearson and Jimmy Greenhoff have won international honours, and Stevie Coppell has gone close enough to stake a claim.

Ireland?—Well, Gerry Daly is a regular for the Republic, and Northern Ireland could field Jimmy Nicholl, Sammy McIlroy, David McCreery and Tommy Jackson.

And Scotland?—There's Alex Forsyth, Martin Buchan, Stewart Houston and myself

. . . and, at a pinch, I've no doubt that manager Tommy Docherty would be willing to turn out, as well! In fact, we had another Scottish international at Old Trafford until last season, when big Jim Holton moved on to Sunderland.

The great thing is that when the players get together on match days, no matter what their nationalities, they're all for one and one for all. In a word, they're United.

And as for the fans who regularly flock in their thousands to Old Trafford and other grounds around the country, when we're playing away, there's only one word to describe them . . . FAN-tastic.

I began my career with Glasgow Celtic, and at that time in my footballing life, I thought there was no crowd to beat the one at Parkhead. In Scotland,

by and large, you support one or other of the "Big Two"—Celtic or Rangers. My team north of the Border was always Celtic . . . even if I did spend the early part of my life in London.

The family moved south when I was a mere nipper, and almost 10 years passed before we returned to Scotland. It was then that I began to play Soccer regularly, and on a competitive basis, too, because the school I attended won virtually every trophy for which we competed. Indeed, seven of that side went on to become professional footballers, so you can imagine how much talent we had in our school team.

I had become a schoolboy international, by the time that Celtic indicated they fancied me. I was 14 years old, and I was invited to train a couple of

Some of the United fans who made the trip to Notts County's ground at Meadow Lane to celebrate their club's promotion to the First Division in April 1975

nights a week at Parkhead. It meant a 30-mile return trip by train, but it was worth it, because I was Celtic-daft—and because, of course, I hoped I would one day wear the famous Celtic jersey as a first-teamer.

I have many happy memories of my days at Parkhead: scoring 14 goals during the first couple of months after I had made the first team; knocking in a hat-trick against Airdrie; scoring the winner in a European Cup quarter-final against the Hungarian side, Ujpest Dosza . . . and the equaliser in the second leg of the tie at Parkhead, with 75,000 people cheering their heads off.

Two years running, I was a marksman in the Scottish Cup

final, and each time Celtic carried off the trophy, and by the time I had ended my days at Parkhead, I had collected winner's medals in the League, the Scottish Cup and the League Cup.

Then I had to make the big decision—which was whether to join Liverpool or Manchester United. Liverpool were heading for the League cham-

pionship and the U.E.F.A. Cup—they won both in season 1972–73—and United, it seemed, were heading for the Second Division.

Well, United did go down—but we bounced straight back. And in our first season back in Division 1, we went all the way to Wembley and were only just pipped for the First Division championship. After beating Derby County in the semi-finals of the F.A. Cup, we lost to Southampton at Wembley, and as we had already lost a vital home League game against Stoke, we knew we were not going to claim the championship, either. Who did?—Liverpool . . . along with the U.E.F.A. Cup again.

So I've known the ups and downs of football and I've learned to take the rough with the smooth. In my early days

Colin Todd gets in his tackle just in time to rob Sammy McIlroy

at Old Trafford I found that things were not going just right, and when a club has spent £200,000 on you, you want to be a success. The trouble was that the role I was playing didn't suit me, and it took quite a while for us to work it out. Eventually, we did get it right, and I began to get among the goals and make my presence felt in midfield.

I had another couple of spells when I wasn't bang in top form, but each time I played my way out of the rough patch and put my game together again, and it's here that I'd like to make a couple of points. First, I may be on the small side—but I'm a fighter. It's when things are not going right that I am at my most determined.

Never for a moment did I have any doubts about my own ability, and I was convinced that, in the end, I would win through.

That's something for you to remember, if you have ideas about becoming a professional footballer. It isn't all glamour and glitter; you've got to put a lot of hard work into it, and be dedicated to the job. I don't smoke or drink, and I don't keep late hours . . . and I believe that this code of living will help me to keep going when others have had to hang

Martin Buchan (left) and Leeds' Joe Jordan in a race for the ball. For Scotland, of course, they are often team-mates.

up their boots.

The second point I want to make is that everyone loves a guy who shows that he's ready to fight back—especially, maybe, if he's no giant in the physical sense. And even when things were not going well for me at Old Trafford, I was always trying my hardest. The fans may have been a bit disappointed by some of my displays at first, but they recognised that I was doing everything I could to set things right and show them I was worth the money United had paid for me.

The fans had to exercise quite a bit of patience, and so did I. But the time came when I started to show everyone the real Lou Macari . . . and I can tell you that no-one gave me greater support than those United fans.

I mentioned the support that Celtic receive from their crowd, and in a way, I suppose it's something when you can say that the fans at a club give you a bit of a hard time of it, when you're on your way elsewhere. That happened to me at Parkhead—but it was a bit of a compliment, really, for those fans were giving rein to their disappointment that I was leaving. They didn't want me to go . . . and I could appreciate their feelings. They still get a crack in now and again, when I go home to Scotland; but I know we understand each other, and that's how it should be.

At Old Trafford, the fans have stuck with United through thick and thin. In the days when we were fighting to avoid the drop into the Second Division, they still rolled up to give us their cheers; and when we were fighting to return to the top flight, our gates were tremendous—those fans

followed us around the country, often doubling or even trebling the usual gate on opponents' grounds. Yes, the Second Division clubs certainly missed us, when we went up!

In the season when we went to Wembley, it was a common thing for us to play in front of almost 60,000 people on our own ground—and many other First Division clubs made their games all-ticket, when United were providing the opposition. I remember when we played at Leeds, and the big car park near the Elland-road ground was packed with cars and coaches—including coaches from places all round the country. And they were all taking Manchester United fans to the game. We even have a fan club in Malta, and manager Tommy Docherty has been over there to meet those supporters.

When he was at Stoke, Jimmy Greenhoff became used to playing in front of an average home gate of just over 20,000—except when United were the visitors. Then the gate was usually doubled. And I know Jimmy appreciates playing in front of the Old Trafford multitude—not to mention being in the same side as brother Brian.

When I look back, in spite of the ups and downs, I am thankful that in my career I have played for two great clubs, and in front of two great sets of supporters. Believe me, a host of cheering fans can help a player raise his game and a team to win matches it might otherwise have lost. So from Lou Macari, here's a vote of thanks to the folk who roll up to watch Manchester United, wherever they play. You may not know me personally, but my team-mates and I really do appreciate the loyalty you have shown to us.

A Dream Come True

Mick Lyons

Mike Lyons holds off the challenge of Chelsea's Ray Wilkins

When you're born in a city like Liverpool or Manchester, there's only one thing you can do, as soon as you're old enough to take an interest in football—and that's to pick sides. I was born on Merseyside, and the team of my choice became Everton. Which was why it gave me such a thrill one day, many years later, when I led out Everton against Queen's Park Rangers at Loftus-road as the skipper. And we topped it off that day by scoring four goals without reply!

I come from a family of true-blue Evertonians, and I can claim to have been a season-ticket holder when I was just eight years old. I used to watch "my" team from a seat in the Gwladys-street stand, in those days . . . and I'll confess that, even then, I used to dream of a day when I might be leading the Everton players out on the park.

I played for my school teams, of course, and I was skipper more often than not; and I used to imagine what it felt like to be Brian Labone, who captained Everton when they won the championship of the First Division. The day came when I played in the same Everton side as "Labby", and eventually, I succeeded him as the skipper. That was a tremendous honour for me.

When I was considerably younger, Everton were always in the thick of the fight for honours, and they usually seemed to be winning something. After I had broken through to First Division football, Everton were striving to repeat that kind of success, and they spent a great deal of money in the process.

I saw some of my old team-mates depart . . . Alan Ball, Howard Kendall, Archie Styles, Gary Jones and John Connolly. I also saw some big-money signings arrive . . . Bob Latchford, Duncan McKenzie and Bruce Rioch, for instance. And always the battle has been to keep Everton in the fore-front of the challenge for honours, because our supporters have been brought up on a diet of success—and good football.

In fact, as an Evertonian in every sense of the word, I would hate to have to choose between playing for England or winning something with Everton—because I suspect I'd have to plump for Everton. That's how much of an Everton supporter I am. At the same time, I recognise that playing well for a club such as Everton is one of the best ways of winning international honours, and I was delighted when Don Revie called me up for the England Under-23 team. So maybe, before I've finished, I shall have the best of both worlds!

Mike Lyons and Spurs' Willie Young seem somewhat worried about the approaching football!

One of the questions people are always asking me is which position I like best. I've played in the centre of the defence, in midfield, and done a job up front on occasion for Everton. Well, I've maintained for a long time that the centre-half spot suits me best . . . but, having said that, I've also got to admit that I really do enjoy playing in midfield, which is the hub of all the action, and getting into a position where I can stick the ball past the opposing 'keeper.

So in a way, I suppose, when I'm not playing at centre-half I've got to prove myself wrong

—because whatever, I want to be in the first team. And playing for Everton is the thing that matters most. By now, perhaps, you'll have got the impression that I'm a true-blue, and you aren't wrong!

It's funny how your career can develop, because in my early days, I started out as a striker, and I didn't do too badly at the job, when I was making my way with Everton reserves. Then along came a lad called David Johnson, and he got my place up front—and I made the switch successfully to centre-half. The funny thing is that David was a Liverpool supporter, before he became a professional footballer at Goodison . . . and he finally joined "his" club when he was transferred from Ipswich to Liverpool for £200,000. So he arrived at Anfield via a round-about route.

I remember one game in particular when I played no fewer than three different roles for Everton during the 90 minutes. It was against Derby County. I started out playing up front; then I moved into the back-four line; then I did a stint in midfield . . . and finally ended up back as a front-line man. That was because circumstances during the match dictated these positional changes, and I can tell you that there were times when I wasn't quite sure what I WAS supposed to be doing.

At one time in my career,

also, criticism used to bother me a bit. I didn't like to hear the fans getting on my back, and I didn't like to read criticism of me in the newspapers. I found that when the fans were having a go, I tended to lose concentration. But when I thought about it all, I realised that the person who was suffering most was myself—so I determined from then on not to take any notice of what people said or wrote.

However, I think that often there is an advantage to be gained from playing away from home, because you're not under the constant scrutiny of your own supporters, and the knowledge that you're up against the bulk of the fans from the start, as well as the team you're playing, tends to make you more determined to succeed. At home, you can easily become afraid of making a mistake, in front of people who want so much to see you winning; but the reverse can apply when you're playing away. Then, it's the opposition who may be worried about making mistakes, and you can sometimes cash in on this.

Because I have played in so many roles, people ask me about the various problems involved, and they also ask who I have found to be the most difficult opponents in direct opposition. So far as playing in defence is concerned, I always had a great deal of respect for the former Tottenham and Scotland player, Alan Gilzean, who used to win the ball in the air so often, and who could play one-touch football brilliantly. He would lay the ball off, and be away in a flash to get the return.

When it comes to facing up to a back-four man myself, I'll say that Derby County and

One of today's strongest defenders —Roy McFarland: seen here playing for England against Scotland in May 1976

England centre-half Roy McFarland takes some beating —and I'll add, of course, that he comes from Merseyside, originally. Roy may look casual, and he can play football—but he's in quickly to the tackle, he's powerful in the air, and he doesn't let you turn. So you find that he's giving you absolutely nothing.

One thing about playing in different positions: you learn how to adapt, and the experience you gain from coming up against some of the best players in the First Division you can utilise to your own advantage, in games to come. You learn how to stop a striker, how to get past a centre-half; how to run things in midfield, and how to clamp down on the opposition there. And, all-round, you become a better player.

I think I've learned something, also, from the various players who have been skipper during my time at Everton—Brian Labone, Alan Ball, Howard Kendall and Roger Kenyon. Brian, Howard and Roger led mainly by example, doing their own jobs quietly and effectively; "Bally" led by example, too—but he was also enthusiastic and bouncy, and that rubbed off on to his teammates, too. I'm the quiet type, but I like to think that I have something to offer, as a leader by example, and by the fact that I have played in so many different roles.

We may not have been among the leading contenders for the championship in season 1976–77, but there were plenty of games in which we showed we could be a match for any other side in the country— not least, when we went to Old Trafford and gave Manchester United a 3-0 beating, to go in against Bolton for a place in the final of the League Cup.

As a team, we have shown that we can make character count, and as a club, Everton have shown that they intend to regain their place as one of the big guns not only in the First Division, but in Europe. The signing of players such as Bob Latchford, Martin Dobson, Duncan McKenzie and Bruce Rioch emphasises that Everton are ready to pay big fees for quality, while they are also ready to snap up bargains like Andy King, and give the home-grown lads their chance.

I'm proud to be a home-grown product, proud to be an Evertonian. And I hope and believe that, given the sort of breaks you need in football, I can lead Everton to success in the coming seasons. I can assure you that if I have MY way, it won't be all Liverpool, when the rest of the country weighs up the Soccer strength of Merseyside.

My Partnership with 'Supermac'

JOHN TUDOR

As seen by millions on television—the superb headed goal by John Tudor playing for Stoke against Ipswich in September 1976

I've had a variety of jobs in my life—I've worked two or three times on building sites, in a wood yard, as a fork-lift truck driver, as an apprentice fitter, and for a floor-tiling firm . . . and, of course, for several seasons I formed a goal-scoring partnership with Malcolm Macdonald. "Supermac", to all his fans.

My footballing travels have taken me from my home town of Ilkeston, near Derby, to Coventry City, Sheffield United, Newcastle United and Stoke City, so in three instances—with the Blades, the Magpies and the Potters—I've got used to wearing Soccer stripes. And I also hope I've won a few stripes in the game, on my own account.

Looking back, it seems that I've had what people might call a chequered career; indeed, at one time, I was becoming convinced that I wasn't going to have a career at all, so far as professional football was concerned. For a start, I had great expectations—I fondly imagined that I was destined to go straight to a club when I left school . . . but that didn't turn out to be the case at all.

When I did leave school, I drifted along doing various jobs, and hung on until I was 17 or 18, in the hope that one day, almost out of the blue, someone would knock on the front door and tell me his club wanted to sign me as a professional. But when I finally got my break, things just didn't happen that way.

I'd landed a job working in a wood yard, and for the first time I felt that here was a career I might carve out for myself (if you'll pardon the pun) outside professional football. At the time, I was playing

Malcolm Macdonald, with both arms raised, has just scored England's first goal against Cyprus at Wembley in 1975. England won 5-0 and Supermac scored them all—a Wembley international record for England.

for Ilkeston Town in the Midland League, and Jim Rayner, who was the manager of Ilkeston Town, went over to Leamington Spa to play in a match which was organised to "christen" the floodlights of Lockheed, a Leamington Sunday League club.

There were three big names from the world of professional football there, that night, all of them from Coventry City.

They were Jimmy Hill, Pat Saward and Alan Dicks, and afterwards, they got talking about football, and they asked Jim Rayner if he knew of any good youngsters who were ready to take the plunge into League football.

It seems that Coventry City —the Sky Blues, as they are affectionately known to their supporters—were looking for a centre-forward aged around

17 who could play for their youth team. Jim gave them my name, and he must have given me a fair recommendation as well, for I went to Coventry for a month. The only snag was that Jim hadn't got my age right—by then, I was 19 years old.

But once I had got to Highfield-road, I made sufficient impact, even though they realised that they couldn't sign me on to play in their Youth Cup side. And, fortunately for me, Coventry were ready to take a chance and willing to experiment. Had I gone to a less go-ahead club, I might still have been waiting for my chance.

But the Sky Blues were soaring up the Second Division, and there was a sense of adventure in everything they did.

They told me I could remain with them as an amateur, or take the plunge and join them as a professional. I was earning £24 a week at the wood yard, and my Soccer wages would be exactly half that amount—but this didn't deter me!

I signed on the dotted line in the January, and my contract extended until the end of

that season. I also had an "insurance policy", because my boss at the wood yard said that if things didn't work out, I could have my old job back.

I suppose that, deep down, I was determined to prove that I could make it as a professional footballer, if only to show a few clubs they should have taken a chance on me. For I had visited Sheffield

Malcolm Macdonald playing for Arsenal against his old club Newcastle United in December 1976. Stewart Barrowclough (right) and Tommy Cassidy are the Newcastle players. 'Supermac' celebrated by scoring a hat-trick in Arsenal's 5-3 win.

United as a 15-year-old, played for a short spell as an amateur with Nottingham Forest, trained with Notts. County and Derby County, played a couple of games for Chesterfield, and for Middlesbrough reserves, too.

But, clearly, at the end of it all, I wasn't good enough to warrant five or six clubs jostling for the privilege of signing me. And really, when Coventry gave me my break, I had begun to think I wasn't going to get into the professional game. Maybe the fact that, when I was 15, I had a long illness held me back a bit; I know that I certainly outgrew my strength, and this didn't help me to impress clubs, even though, in those days, I was playing as an orthodox winger, and not as a striker whose job it was to go in where it really hurt.

Well, Coventry offered me a new contract, at the end of my first season, and I broke through to the first team when I'd been at Highfield-road around nine months. I'd been scoring goals in the reserves, so they felt the gamble of promoting me was justified.

By then, I was strong enough to meet the challenge, and I'd been playing in the Midland League against fellows who were considerably older than me. So playing for Coventry reserves, with youngsters, was easier in one way.

I almost helped the Sky Blues gain promotion in my first season as a Second Division player—we finished third —and 12 months later, I was collecting a Second Division championship medal, as Coventry and Wolves went up. Then, after two and a half years at Highfield-road, I was transferred for £65,000 to . . .

Sheffield United, the club where, as a 15-year-old, I had first had ideas about becoming a professional.

For two years I played for the Blades, and became their leading marksman, which encouraged Newcastle United to offer £67,000 for me. And that was another big step in my career, for Newcastle had so many big-name players, including established internationals. They had traded two players and paid cash, as well, to land me, so they must have thought I was up to standard.

By then, I'd done all my worrying—enough to last a lifetime—and I was ready for the challenge. Football is big business, and it has its pitfalls, but it's still a game, and I had reached the stage where I was playing for the sheer enjoyment of it all, as well as for wages. And, of course, it was at Newcastle where I teamed up with "Supermac", when he was signed from Luton. He was the best thing that ever happened to me in football.

People can say what they like about Malcolm Macdonald; I only know that we suited each other very well. And I'm not too big to admit that it was he who put me on the map, for we formed a partnership in which goals—dozens of them—were the end-product.

We had three or four seasons together, and each season saw us sticking away between 20 and 30 goals between us. I think I did a fair amount for him, and I know he appreciated this—even if I did stop being his room-mate, because he snored! "Supermac" is an extrovert, but he can afford to be—because he makes good his promise, and that is to score goals. He scored them

for Newcastle, and he's carried on scoring them for Arsenal.

I remember a game against Queen's Park Rangers at Loftus-road. We won 4-1— he scored three of the goals, and I got the other. In fact, we seemed to be a bit of a bogy side for Rangers.

I remember a game we lost, too—Ipswich beat us 4-3 on their ground. The boot was on the other foot that time, and not just because of the score-line. I got two of our goals, and Malcolm hit the other.

But our partnership really was something special, and we made a lot of goals for each other. One game in which I was happy not to score was the 1974 F.A. Cup semi-final against Burnley. I'm not saying it was a great match, but Malcolm came up with a couple of goals that took us to Wembley—in fact, I think it's true to say that his goals were fantastic efforts . . . and yet, otherwise, he never got a kick! For the rest of us, those goals apart, the game turned out to be a real battle, and Iam McFaul, who kept goal for Newcastle then, was unbeatable.

Malcolm and I, I like to think, were like brothers. We got on well together, on and off the park. We lunched together, talked football together, shared many a laugh together. I went to his going-away party, when he left for Arsenal, and it was a bit of a heartbreak occasion for both of us. And although I'm now a Stoke player, and there will be no quarter asked or given, when we're in opposition, I'll always be glad that we were team-mates, and I wish "Supermac" every success— except, of course, when Stoke play Arsenal!

WHEN YOUR SLIP IS SHOWING

Colin Todd

Dismay for the England players and joy for the Scots after an own goal had made the score 2-0 for Scotland in the 1974 match at Hampden Park

Twenty-two players are in position and ready for the kick-off—one of them with the ball at his feet. The referee is ready—he has a last quick glance around the pitch, a look towards each of his linesmen, a check on his watch. Then he starts the game—and if he is that popular Welsh referee, Clive Thomas, he not only pushes at the air with his hand as if he was starting some vehicle on a downhill run, he gives a kick as if to remind the player with the ball at his feet that Mr Thomas is waiting for him to set the ball rolling.

Then, except perhaps for a stoppage if a player is badly injured, it is action all the way for the players. Maybe one or other, maybe both, of the keepers have their moments of comparative inactivity but for the other players it is involvement all the time. Yet—and I think it was a television glimpse of a player's face on

my screen not long ago that made me think of this—there are perhaps two possible moments of loneliness for a player during a match. There is an old saying about the worse loneliness being the loneliness in a large crowd.

Two moments—one of them I am mainly guessing at because I have not had much experience of it. But imagine the loneliness of the player stepping up to take a penalty kick—particularly one late in an important match that could decide the result. Sometimes, but not often, he runs up to an accompaniment of boos. But usually there is a sort of hush around the ground and he—and the keeper—are about to wage their individual contest in what is overall essentially a team game. The spotlight is on the kicker. There will be applause and relief if he scores but also a feeling that he *ought* to score. The keeper is more fortunate—a

47

Chris Nicholl (right)—the man who scored all four goals in a two-all draw!—seen here in action for Villa against Everton's Bob Latchford

hero if he saves and not likely to be blamed if he doesn't!

Small wonder that I expect you have all seen, live or on television, matches when a penalty has been awarded and no one has seemed very eager to come up and take it!

And nowadays the ability of players to score from the penalty spot is becoming of ever greater importance with the possibility of major international and inter-club matches being decided by penalty kicks if the scores after extra-time are level. Will we ever forget the dramatic finale to the European Football Championship Final in Belgrade between Czechoslovakia and the holders West Germany?

The normal match had been dramatic enough with the Czechoslovaks two goals up in the first half-hour; a West German goal before half-time but then no more scoring until the very last minute of normal time when—echoes of the famous Wembley 1966 World Cup Final —West Germany snatched an equaliser. There was no further score during extra-time for two very tired teams—both of whom had been involved in semi-final matches that had gone to extra-time only a few days before. So the score remained two-all and the stage was set for the penalty-kicking deciders.

Not a sudden death contest but, in its first stage, one between five players of each side. If the number of successful conversions were the same, then other players would have to continue.

Masny first for the Czechoslovaks—a goal; Bonhof for the Germans 1-1; Nehoda 2-1; Flohe 2-2; Ondrus 3-2; Bongartz 3-3; Jurkemik 4-3; Hoeness—a miss and then the heat was really on Panenka for Czechoslovakia. If he scored the Czechoslovaks had won; if he missed then the fifth West German would have a chance of again levelling the score. Would that fifth one have been their skipper Franz Beckenbauer? I think most of us would have expected the captain to have taken one of the nerve-wracking penalties. Whether or not it was Beckenbauer's turn next we were never to know since Panenka, very coolly with a precisely placed but not hard shot, scored and brought the European Championship to Czechoslovakia.

And, as is always likely when football's the subject, I seem to have wandered from my point—those *two* lonely moments. As I said, I am not usually asked to step up and take a penalty. Nor, thankfully, have I often experienced what I think is the most wretched of lonely moments—the one shown on that face I glimpsed on the screen after the player had put the ball in his own net!

Own goals come in many shapes and sizes. Some from completely involuntary deflections. As a matter of fact quite a number of goals come from deflected shots with the keeper rightly moving to where the ball should be travelling from the opponent's shot and the ball just striking a defender enough to make it deviate from that predicted course. Nobody thinks of these as own goals and there is often conjecture as to whether other deflections should count as own goals. The generally adopted line of thinking is that if the ball from the attacker's kick would have been on target, then the kicker is credited with the goal he deserves. If however the ball was off target and only went into the net because of the deflection, however unintentional, then it is an own goal.

I see I've let that word *unintentional* creep in. But of course all own goals are unintentional! What I mean is that there is a difference between the player who, thinking the keeper is ready behind him, kicks the ball towards his own goal; and the player who, in a crowded goalmouth is hit by a hard crossed ball.

Either way—but the more so when the own goal has come from a mistake, a misunderstanding—there is a sudden sick feeling about an own goal. Even the fortunate attackers don't seem to know how to salute their lucky goal. Football, as I have already mentioned, is a team game and the ideal goal, the one that brings with it the most satisfaction, is the one in which several players have been involved. The keeper throws the ball out to a back; the back moves forward a few yards, sees a midfield player moving clear towards him; passes the ball to him and straight away starts a run down the wing. Opponents see the back's break and instinctively move to counter it. The midfield player thereupon sends a long pass across the field to the point furthest from the overlapping back. Another of the attackers picks up the ball from the pass and makes straight for the bye line. Opponents, already in some confusion by the feinted overlap, quickly change direction to cut off the new line of attack but your player with the ball pulls it back into the path of a fellow-striker who, with the goal directly before him, can pick his spot to beat the keeper.

No doubt about the spontaneous reaction of the players to such a goal. The actual scorer naturally takes most of the back-slapping but every member of the team wants to do something to show his delight.

But what do you do when it is an opponent who has shot the ball into his own back, passing back to a keeper who wasn't there?

That's the lonely, sick moment for the unlucky player who wishes then he was a hundred miles away whilst his team-mates don't know

Mick Mills (No. 3) reaches the ball narrowly ahead of Derby's Charlie George

whether to swear at him or to sympathise—and generally they let him walk away and leave it to him to forget it and concentrate on the game again. Maybe too his team-mates realise that the same thing may happen to them some day! And I am not saying that because I recall the 1974 match against Scotland at Hampden Park! The Scots won 2-0 and *their* goals were scored by Pejic and Todd!

I suppose the only crumb of comfort for Mike Pejic and me was that the match was being played at Hampden and not at Wembley. But an own goal at Wembley was what happened to the Charlton Athletic's right-half, Turner, during the 1946 F.A. Cup Final—the first Final when serious competitive football was resumed after the Second World War. Charlton, then a First Division club of course, were playing Derby County as a matter of fact and Turner's own goal was the first goal scored in the match.

In his *History of the F.A. Cup*, Geoffrey Green, wrote: "Do you remember the horror on Turner's face as he turned the ball over his own goal-line to give Derby the lead nine minutes from the end?"

But that was not the end of the story because, as Geoffrey Green continued: "And his (that is Turner's) joy 60 seconds later when he slashed a free-kick outside the penalty-area into a forest of Derby's legs, whence it emerged at a tangent to slide past Woodley into the net?"

So, H. Turner twice got his name on the score-sheet for the 1946 Cup Final—once for each side; and it is remarkable how often it does happen that a player scores both for his own side and for his opponents in the same match.

Last season had barely got under way before on 28 August 1976 the match results included these two:

Nottingham Forest 1 Wolves 3
(*Daley* o.g.) (Gould 2, *Daley*)
Crewe 3 Hartlepools 1
(Purdie, Davies, (*Lugg* o.g.)
Lugg pen.)

In those two matches the own goals had no effect on the result but they did a month later when Paul Mariner, before his transfer to Ipswich, after nodding Plymouth into the lead against Bolton, moved down to help his defence and scored the goal that gave Bolton a one-all draw—and maybe the point that at the end of the season could put them back into the First Division! And on the same Saturday—25 September 1976 as a matter of fact, Colin

Franks was doing the same thing, scoring both goals in Sheffield United's home one-all draw with Blackburn.

Still those one goal at each end incidents fall short of what happened when Aston Villa and Leicester met in March 1976. The score was two-all and Chris Nicholl scored all four goals.

Pat Kruse of Torquay United was responsible for a remarkable own goal during the New Year holiday matches in 1977. Playing at home, Torquay kicked off against Cambridge United and before a Cambridge player had touched the ball, unlucky Pat Kruse had put the ball into his own net.

And that you may think is something of a record. Well, it *shares* a record, for according to the record books Alan Mullery, playing for Fulham against Sheffield Wednesday, did the same thing back in 1961.

You need to go back further than 1961 to see another player scoring four goals—two for each side—in a match, as I mentioned Chris Nicholl doing in March 1976. The books say that in 1923, playing for Oldham against Manchester United in a Second Division match, a left-back named Wynne did the same thing.

The record books also, incidentally, mention one of the oddest of all own goals, scored for Chelsea when they were playing Leicester at Stamford Bridge in 1954. Two Leicester players reached for the ball and connected with it simultaneously to send it into their own net. So the score was recorded as "Milburn and Froggatt, shared own goal".

Jack Froggatt, of course, had been a free-scoring winger for Portsmouth when they won the championship in two successive seasons. Later he played at centre-half—he played for England in both positions—but never forgot his former attacking role. And that reminds me of the most remarkable 1976 example of the same player scoring for both sides. It happened in the semi-final of the European Football Championship between Czechoslovakia and the Netherlands. That splendid centre defender of the national side and of Slovan Bratislava, Anton Ondrus, had given the Czechoslovaks the lead in the 19th minute then, a quarter of an hour from time, he put in his own goal to equalise for the Dutch. I expect he, more than any other player, was relieved when his side won 3-1 in extra time. They went on, as I have already mentioned, to win the European Football Championship.

SINGIN' THE BLUES

Joe Royle

I've known plenty of ups and downs in football, but the one thing that has remained constant is the fact that I'm still singin' the Blues! For when I left the Blues of Everton, the club I had joined straight from school, it was to become one of the Maine-road Blues, with Manchester City. And that made Christmas, 1974, one of the most important dates of my life.

On the morning of Christmas Eve, I was playing in a five-a-side game at Bellefield, the training headquarters of Everton. Things hadn't been going too well for me for quite a while, and I must admit that I wasn't anticipating the sort of expensive Christmas present which Manchester City had been planning. For they had decided that I was worth £160,000 . . .

There I was, giving it all I'd got in this five-a-side, and suddenly there was Billy Bingham, then the manager of Everton, giving me a shout and telling me that Manchester City and Everton had agreed terms for my transfer. So it was up to me. I didn't waste a second . . . I went into the dressing-room, had a quick bath and got changed, and then I was on my way to talk to City manager Tony Book at Maine-road. In fact, I made a short stop on the way, to phone my wife.

At that time, of course, she was completely unaware of the developments that had taken place that morning, and I couldn't stay on the phone more than a minute or two. But I had already made up my mind that I was going to jump at the chance of this transfer, and I told her that no matter what, I was going to become a Manchester City player that day.

Two hours after Billy Bingham had called me on one side, I had become a Manchester City player, and was being told that my name would go up on the team sheet for the Boxing Day match against—guess who?—Liverpool, at Anfield! They, of course, are Everton's greatest rivals, and I had played in some thrilling derby games in the past. I'd like to say that I made a story-book debut for Manchester City—I'd like to say that, but the sad truth is that Liverpool beat us. Still, there's always a next time . . . I hope!

Naturally, I felt somewhat sad at leaving Everton, because this was the club I had always supported as a youngster; this was the club which had given me my first taste of First Division football, when I was only a 16-year-old; and I had had some tremendous times there. I was a member of Everton's F.A. Cup-final side at Wembley in 1968, when they had lost by the only goal against West Brom; I had helped Everton celebrate their League-championship triumph a few seasons later . . . and I had shared their tears when, in 1971, they were pipped in the semi-finals of the F.A. Cup by Liverpool.

I had also gained international recognition, while I was a player at Goodison Park, and that reminds me

A scissors-kick by Denis Tueart for Manchester City against Q.P.R. in October 1976. It did not score but the picture brings back memories of the similar Tueart effort that did count—and brought Manchester City their Football League Cup Final victory over Newcastle United

once again that in football, there are the low points, as well as the highlights. I remember March, 1971, for this provided me with a bitter-sweet experience. I had gone with Everton to play against Panathinaikos in the European Cup, in Greece, and we returned home sadly, after defeat. I learned then that my son, Lee Joseph, had been born as the game was being played. And then Liverpool won that Old Trafford Cup semi-final . . .

I had a spell when I spent a long time on my back, and I know that there were people who felt that my career in top-class football could be at an end. It needed an operation and a great deal of effort to get back to full fitness, afterwards, and even then there was the question of regaining the form which had brought me to the notice of the England team manager.

As a matter of fact, although I did come back and began scoring goals for Everton again, things never really seemed to be going for me, after that back trouble, and by the time I was transferred to Manchester City, I was beginning to feel that a change of club might well bring me that vital change of luck.

It didn't look like it, when I went with City to Anfield and we lost on my debut day, and there was a period in my career at Maine-road when I couldn't seem to hit the target, no matter how hard I tried. I must admit that at the time, I was starting to worry a bit about this, because when you're a striker, you're supposed to get goals, and Manchester City had paid a hefty sum of money for me. Not only that, they had shown that they had faith in me—and what a relief it was, when I started to repay them with a few goals.

You cannot score goals to order, you know, and when you're missing chances or not even getting into scoring positions, you begin to worry about your game. When the goals start flowing, you can go through a purple patch where it seems that you cannot miss. I've had experience of both these things, but the main factor is that I honestly believe I have done a good job for Manchester City, even when I haven't been tucking all the scoring chances away.

Football is still very much a team game, and if you're playing your part by working hard, not just for yourself, but for the rest of the lads, you can go home after the match feeling contented.

City, of course, have a team loaded with talent—England internationals in men like Joe Corrigan, Mike Doyle, Dave Watson, Dennis Tueart and Brian Kidd, Scotland stars such as Asa Hartford and Willie Donachie . . . and many of them have known what it is to fight back after rough spells. Joe Corrigan had to win over the supporters who used to be on his back . . . Asa Hartford knew what it was to miss out on a transfer from West Brom to Leeds, after an adverse

Brian Kidd in action for Manchester City. His partnership with Joe Royle increasingly flourished as the 1976–77 season moved on. So too did the great promise of Gary Owen (seen right in the picture)

medical report . . . and Brian Kidd had to prove himself all over again, when he returned to Manchester from Arsenal.

"Kiddo" had been a long-time favourite with the Manchester United fans, and he made a hit when he joined Arsenal. But when he returned to Manchester to play for City, he found himself going through a patch when the goals just weren't coming and, like me, he gritted his teeth and carried on working at his game, until the goal-den touch came back.

Dennis Tueart had to justify a huge transfer fee after he left Sunderland for Maine-road, and this isn't always easy. But Dennis, who was one of Sunderland's heroes when they won the F.A. Cup in 1973, soon showed that he intended to carry on scoring goals and turning defenders inside-out, and he is one of the crowd favourites at City.

Yes, for some of us it's been a long haul, at times, and no-one knows this more than Colin Bell, who spent more than a year on the sidelines after being injured in a derby game against Manchester United. Colin missed out on England matches, too—he would have been an automatic choice —and City also missed his inspiring example, and his sheer strength, as well as skill.

When you come to think of it, Manchester City as a whole have had to recover from some setbacks—for instance, there was a time, a couple of seasons ago, when the Maine-road Blues couldn't seem to win a match away from home.

Last season, things switched round, for we picked up points on tour as though we had been doing it all our lives, and we kept up with the challengers for the championship—largely thanks to our displays in away

Grim determination shows on their faces as Kenny Burns tackles Joe Royle

games. I remember going to Leeds on Boxing Day, 1976, and Brian Kidd was the man who stuck two goals past the Leeds 'keeper, to register victory for City and close the gap between ourselves and Ipswich and Liverpool. They were at home on the Boxing Day, too, and they showed character themselves, by coming back from a run of three defeats in four matches and beating Stoke 4-0.

Since I joined City, I've resumed my career in top-class football and gone to Wembley to collect a League Cup-winner's medal—remember that spectacular overhead kick which brought Dennis Tueart a goal?—and I've also been chosen to play for England again.

That reminds me of another disappointment—the World Cup qualifying match which

we lost against Italy in Rome. But I'm philosophical enough now to realise that it's when you have setbacks that you show your real character . . . and that you can overcome them and get back on the rails.

Manchester City have done this, and they have had to compete with Manchester United, as well as the rest of the First Division outfits. I know what it's like, living in a city which is divided in its Soccer loyalties. Once, it was Everton and Liverpool, now it's City and United. And while, as I said, it was a wrench at the time to leave Goodison Park, after all the seasons I had played there, at least I had no problems in recognising my new team-mates. For City and Everton both wear blue . . . and I hope I'll be singing the Maine-road Blues for a long time to come!

SOCCER North American Style

J.M. Jeffery

The Game is the same the World over, but sometimes the name means something different. Be it football, fussball, futbal, etc., whatever the language, to most Europeans it means a game played by kicking a spherical ball. Admittedly some in Britain deviously insist on calling the handling game played with the oval ball "football", forgetting that rugby evolved out of the round ball game. However, in North America things are different. Football means crash-helmeted giants, swollen with layers of padding, hurling a pint-sized rugby ball and their opponents around an artificial grass pitch criss-crossed by a multitude of assorted markings, lines, numbers, club badges, etc., surrounded by ecstatic mini-skirted majorettes, and a crowd that seems to spend most of its time eating pop-corn, or gorging enormous hot-dogs, a papaburger, a mamaburger, or a teenburger, depending on your size, or rather the size of your stomach. Our football is "SOCCER" to the North American, and in both Canada and the United States soccer is making rapid strides in popularity, both from a playing and a spectating point of view. Perhaps the day is not so far away when we may see a repeat of that

shock result of the 1950 World Cup, England 0 United States of America 1.

Here in England you can go and watch United, Rovers, City, or Athletic; in North America it's Aztecs, Rowdies, Jaws, or Earth-quakes. These teams with the exotic names play in the recently very successful North American Soccer League, NASL for short. The roots of soccer go deep in some parts of North America. St. Louis in the States has long been a stronghold of amateur soccer, but in most places it has been the example of the NASL that has led to the recent soccer playing boom, to the extent that in Atlanta in the Deep South, long a hot-bed of American football, more youngsters are playing soccer than either baseball or American football. In Canada too, in cities like Toronto and Vancouver, soccer has caught on in a big way with vast numbers of boys playing for junior clubs in junior leagues on Saturdays and Sundays just as they do here. Those of you who play football for your school team or local junior side might be very interested to read the following account I received in January this year (the middle of the amateur and youth soccer season in North America, but the close

The Geographical Distribution of the NASL Clubs

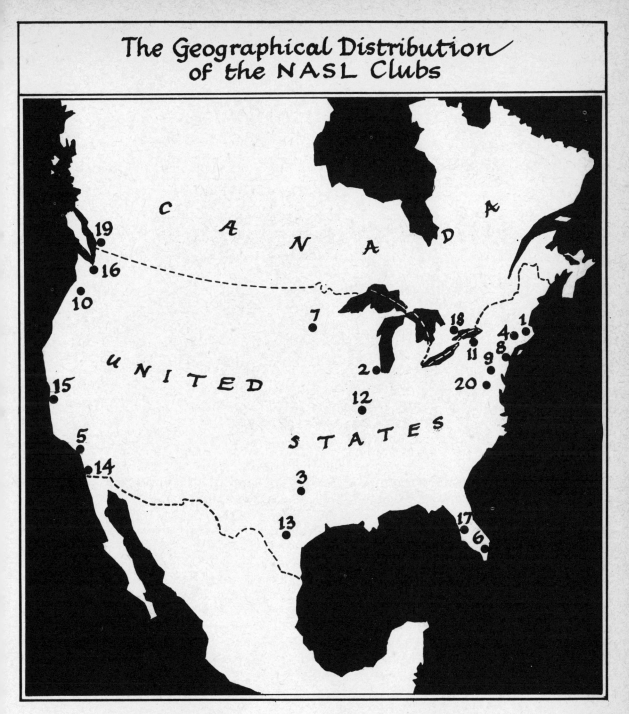

1 Boston Minutemen	11 Rochester Lancers
2 Chicago Sting	12 St. Louis Stars
3 Dallas Tornado	13 San Antonio Thunder
4 Hartford Bicentennials	14 San Diego Jaws
5 Los Angeles Aztecs	15 San Jose Earthquakes
6 Miami Toros	16 Seattle Sounders
7 Minnesota Kicks	17 Tampa Bay Rowdies
8 New York Cosmos	18 Toronto Metros
9 Philadelphia Atoms	19 Vancouver Whitecaps
10 Portland Timbers	20 Washington Diplomats

season for the NASL) from a fifteen-year-old footballer, John Maguire, of West 5th Avenue, Vancouver in Canada. John wrote . . .

"The team I play for plays Sunday afternoons. Our team is the West Point Grey Rangers, Division II, Community. In Division II Community there are 5 teams. It varies every year. Last year we had 8 but 3 folded. Each team plays the other teams 4 or 5 times each.

"The league is divided into divisions by age. The youngest is House League, then Divisions 7, 6, 5, 4, 3, 2 and one. You play in Division 1 for two years, playing both teams in Division 1 first year and second year. There are other teams organized for boys five years and up, also some girls teams.

"Each area such as West Point Grey, Grandview etc. have two teams in each division, one team in 'Community' and one in 'Vancouver and District'. In 'Community' you play teams from Vancouver itself. The Vancouver and District teams play teams from Vancouver and the other Vancouver neighbouring districts (Richmond, West Vancouver, North Vancouver etc.). Divisions 7 to 3 play on Saturdays, Divisions 2 and 1 play on Sundays.

"The League has nothing to do with the school league. Our area may include several schools so the kids can come from any school to play. Each year there are 3 major trophies: the league title, which is for the team with the most points at the end of the season; the Moyes Cup, which is a play-off of the first to fourth place teams; and the Provincial Cup, which involves all of British Columbia.

"We also have practice on Tuesday nights in a Community Centre Gym. We play 4 on 4 with hockey nets and no goalie. It is good for ball control and passing. We also work on shooting, skills, etc.

"Each team has a coach and a general manager. These are volunteer adults, usually parents. The G.M. arranges transportation to away games etc. We have no team bus so parents have to drive us to the games.

"This year we will be going to Seattle to play against an American team. They will then come to Vancouver to play us. As the season stacks right now, we are in third place with a 6 and 3 record, one win behind second place 'South Slope'. Last year we came second and won the Moyes Cup, we hope to do the same this year . . ."

No doubt the success of Vancouver's NASL professional side, the Whitecaps, has had a lot

An incident in American Soccer - note number 17?

to do with the increase in the number of boys and youths like John Maguire who now regularly play soccer in British Columbia. In their early days many of the NASL teams were virtually composed solely of foreign imported players from Europe and South America. However, more recently native born North Americans are taking their rightful place in the professional set-up. In summer 1976 when Vancouver Whitecaps held the touring Glasgow Rangers and Manchester United to 2-2 and 0-0 draws, and beat the West Germans, Borussia Moenchengladbach 4-3, despite the presence of Bertie Vogts, Rainer Bonhof, Jupp Heynckes, and Wolfgang Kleff, they fielded a side that included the likes of Wolves' Phil Parkes, Middlesbrough's Tony McAndrew, and Tommy Ord formerly of Chelsea, New York Cosmos, and Rochester Lancers, but also many players like Brian Robinson, Gary Thompson, Brian Budd, Glen Johnson, Bob and Silvano Lenarduzzi, Bruce Wilson, and Greg Weber who were all products of local British Columbian football. Yes, soccer in North America is certainly on the move.

The North American Soccer League was formed in 1968 as a result of a merger between the two rival professional leagues that were established the previous year, the United States Association, recognised by the World football governing body F.I.F.A., and the outlawed National Professional Soccer League. Seventeen teams competed in the NASL's first season, Atlanta Chiefs capturing the title with a 3-0 victory over San Diego Toros after a 0-0 draw in San Diego. However, the first season was not a success financially, with very small gates forcing many clubs to go bust.

1969 saw a reduced number of teams in the League, but a higher standard of play, and a commitment to attack. In winning the championship Kansas City Spurs hit 53 goals in 16 games, while Kaizer Motaung of Atlanta Chiefs led the league scoring chart with 16 goals in 16 games, not bad going at all. Gates gradually got larger, but league expansion was slow. Newcomers Rochester Lancers took the title in 1970, and a year later Dallas Tornado pipped Atlanta Chiefs. 1972 saw the emergence of New York Cosmos who were to hit world headlines in 1975 by signing Pelé. In 1973 nine teams competed in the League and a record crowd of 18,824 saw Philadelphia Atoms beat Dallas Tornado 2-0 in the final.

During the professional close season, in December 1973, the League expanded considerably, re-establishing itself as a truly national league covering the continent coast to coast, with teams from Los Angeles, San Francisco, Seattle, and Vancouver entering. The 1974 season proved to be the most successful to date in the League's history with over a million spectators watching the matches, an average of nearly 8,000 a game, (in 1971 the average had been merely 3,800). San Jose topped the attendances with an average of 16,500, followed by Seattle (13,700), Philadelphia (11,700), and Vancouver (10,000). Los Angeles Aztecs took the Championship by beating Miami Toros 4-3 on a tie-breaker (3-3 at full-time . . . according to NASL rules the team who scores first in extra-time wins). The Championship Game was watched by 15,500 and given nationwide coverage on CBS television.

1975 was another boom year for the NASL. A crowd of over 21,000 saw Pelé's debut for New York Cosmos, while a League record crowd of 35,600 saw him play in Washington. Tampa Bay Rowdies took the Final 2-0 against Portland Timbers at San Jose, Clyde Best getting the vital second goal. 1976 saw another Best, George, appear on the North American scene with Los Angeles Aztecs. Twenty teams made up the League for the summer '76 season, split into two "Conferences", the Pacific and Atlantic. Each Conference was divided into two geographical sections . . .

Western Division Pacific
Minnesota Kicks
Portland Timbers
St. Louis Stars
Seattle Sounders
Vancouver Whitecaps

Southern Division Pacific
Dallas Tornados
Los Angeles Aztecs
San Antonio Thunder
San Diego Jaws
San Jose Earthquakes

Eastern Division Atlantic
Miami Toros
New York Cosmos
Philadelphia Atoms
Tampa Bay Rowdies
Washington Diplomats

Northern Division Atlantic
Boston Minutemen
Chicago Sting
Hartford Bicentennials
Rochester Lancers
Toronto Metros

Each team played a total of 24 league games, playing each of the teams in its Conference twice, and six of the teams from the other Conference once. League tables are drawn up on the basis of the four geographical divisions, the top three teams in each division going into the final stages. In the first round of the finals the team finishing runners-up in each division plays at home to the team finishing third. The winners of these games play away in the quarter-finals to the divisional champions, and then follows the semi-final and final to find the eventual NASL champions.

All in all the NASL looks set to stay in North America and is beginning to rival American and Canadian football, baseball, and ice hockey, both in terms of numbers playing and watching. Georg N. Meyers, Sports Editor of the Seattle Times, noted with some surprise that while Tampa Bay Buccaneers were beating Atlanta Falcons 17-3 in the National Football League (the crash-helmeted, oval-ball game) before just 11,000 spectators, a crowd of over 17,000 watched Tampa Bay's soccer team, the Rowdies, play Portland Timbers. Yes, soccer has certainly come to stay in the North American continent. And here's a thought to leave you with. Will we soon be hearing such strange terms as "shut-outs" (a side not conceding a goal during a match), "assists" (laying on a goal for another player), "the blue line" (an off-side area similar to that tried here in the Watney Cup a few years back), and "tie-breakers"? I don't know. Certainly one thing can be said, North Americans like success, and no-one there will be satisfied until Canada and the United States make it to the World Cup finals!

£1,000 ---- NOW IT'S £350,000
by Harry Stanley

Arsenal's David O'Leary (left) and Liam Brady combine to check Duncan McKenzie—playing for Leeds in December 1975. Within a year Duncan had been transferred to Anderlecht and then transferred back to England with Everton

GOING UP . . . that's not just the catch-phrase of the man who operates the lift in the big department store; it's the indicator which shows how the transfer market has spiralled, when clubs have gone out to do their shopping for players. For, just as the housewife has found when she goes to buy the bread and the groceries, the laws of supply and demand have operated in a similar way in Soccer.

Sometimes, as the saying goes, you can't get something for love or money; and in football, you cannot always get the player you want for money alone. You may have to trade one of your own stars, plus cash, to get the superstar YOU want.

The first £1,000 transfer fee changed hands back in the good old days, when the £ in your pocket was really worth £1. A player called Alf Common moved from Sunderland to Middlesbrough, and that was in February, 1905. But see how the money has gone round, since, as clubs have pitched in with staggering sums to land the players they felt were too good to miss.

The first £100,000 player was Alan Ball, who set a record between British clubs when he was signed by Everton from Blackpool. In fact, Everton paid the Seasiders £116,000 for his transfer. That was straight cash, in 1966—and Ball later moved to Arsenal for almost double that amount, then left Highbury for Southampton for something like £60,000. Which brought the total paid for him in just three moves to close on £400,000.

If Ball became the first £100,000 player, Allan Clarke was the first to take a transfer fee to the £150,000 mark, when he joined Leicester

City from Fulham in 1968. Again, it was a cash deal, and Clarke's value shot up once more when he moved on to Leeds, who paid a reputed £165,000 for the England international striker.

It was Martin Peters who broke the £200,000 barrier, when he moved in 1970—two years after Clarke had joined Leicester—and the deal between West Ham and Tottenham signalled a different kind of transfer, for Jimmy Greaves went from Spurs to the Hammers, in part-exchange.

Leicester City figured in the big-money transfer market again, this time as sellers, when they accepted an offer of £250,000 from ambitious Derby County for David Nish, and that was straight cash. It happened in 1972, and Nish was the first player to be rated as a quarter-of-a-million-pound man here.

In 1973, Manchester City set a record for goalkeepers, when they signed Keith McRae from Motherwell. He became the first £100,000 goalkeeper. There came a day when he lost his place through injury and Joe Corrigan, a 'keeper who had cost City nothing, nailed down the first-team spot so well that McRae, after a season or more of soldiering on in the reserves, decided he wanted to leave Maine-road and seek first-team football elsewhere.

In 1974, there came a deal which really made headlines . . . Birmingham striker Bob Latchford became a £350,000 player, when he moved to Everton. In fact, it wasn't all cash that changed hands, for Howard Kendall and Archie Styles left Goodison to join the St. Andrew's club.

In 1974, also, Bruce Rioch joined Derby County from Aston Villa, and—at £200,000—he became the first player from the Second Division to command such a transfer fee. It was straight cash, too. And in the same year, Manchester City and Sunderland agreed on a £375,000 deal, when Tony Towers moved to Roker Park, and Dennis Tueart and Mick Horswill joined the Maine-road club. The valuation of Tueart was £250,000 . . . which made him the top-priced player to move from a Second Division club.

By then, the business of paying cash and swapping players, as well, had become the Soccer style, and when Dave Watson left Roker Park to join Tueart at Maine-road, young centre-half Jeff Clarke travelled in the opposite direction.

Of course, there were still massive cash transfers, and Stoke City figured in three of them.

Alan Ball in action for Southampton against Millwall in January 1977. Previously Alan Ball had featured in big transfer deals—from Blackpool to Everton, and from Everton to Arsenal. But Alan's whole-hearted endeavours have always stayed the same . . .

They spent almost three-quarters of a million pounds on three players—Peter Shilton, Alan Hudson, and Geoff Salmons. Shilton was valued at around £330,000, Hudson at £240,000, and Salmons at £180,000. Hudson later left Stoke for Arsenal, and the Potteries club got something like £200,000 of their money back.

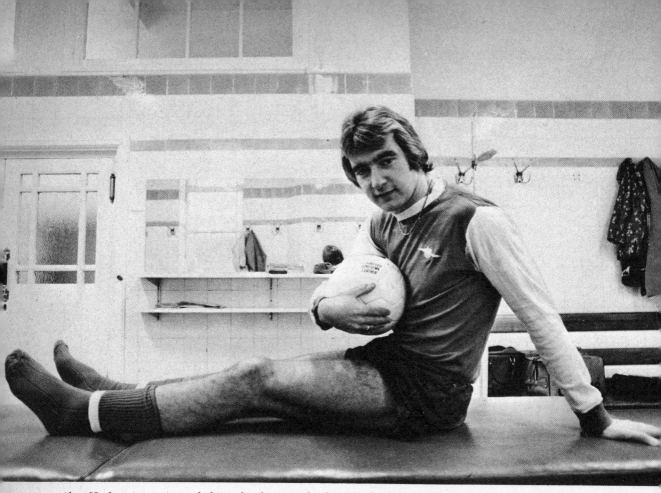

Alan Hudson in an Arsenal shirt after his transfer from Stoke City. It was a return to London for Alan Hudson whose career had begun with Chelsea.

Meanwhile, Rioch left Derby County, too—and joined Everton, in a £180,000 cash deal. Also signed by Everton was Duncan McKenzie, who had cost Leeds £200,000, and been transferred to Anderlecht, of Belgium, for a similar fee. Everton, indeed, have been one of the game's biggest spenders, in their bid to achieve success.

They spent £140,000 on Mick Bernard, £300,000 on Martin Dobson, but a mere £35,000 on Andy King. They also got around £200,000 back when they transferred Gary Jones and John Connolly to Birmingham.

If Everton and Sunderland have been among the game's biggest spenders in recent seasons, you cannot exclude Manchester United and Manchester City—or Liverpool. And if you want an example of one of the game's shrewdest sellers, you need look no further than Burnley.

Manchester United spent a fortune in a few months: Alex Forsyth, Jim Holton, Lou Macari, Mick Martin, Gerry Daly, George Graham . . . they arrived in quick succession, and it meant United had laid out around half a million

pounds in a matter of weeks. They had also paid big money for Martin Buchan, and later were to spend £70,000 on Gordon Hill, sign Stuart Pearson in a £200,000 deal, and transfer £120,000 straight cash to Stoke City in exchange for Jimmy Greenhoff.

Manchester City's spending has been on a massive scale, too. Dennis Tueart, Dave Watson, Asa Hartford, Joe Royle, Brian Kidd . . . there wasn't much change out of one million pounds, when this parade of Soccer talent had been assembled.

Burnley are the club who have made an outstanding success of the policy of selling to survive, and remain in competition with the big-city clubs. In the past 12 months, Burnley have felt the chill wind of the economic storm, but over the years, they have dealt more shrewdly than most in the transfer market, especially on the selling side. Willie Morgan and John Connelly were sold to Manchester United for six-figure fees; Martin Dobson and Leighton James each brought £300,000, when they joined Everton and Derby County, respectively. And there were other, lesser sales.

On the buying side, Burnley extended themselves when they paid Bolton a club-record fee of £60,000 for striker Paul Fletcher, and they topped that figure by going close to £100,000 when they signed winger Tony Morley from Preston. But their outlay has been far overshadowed by the money they have raked in—more than £2,000,000, through the years, for players whom they had groomed for stardom.

Stoke City got most of their money back, when they sold Alan Hudson to Arsenal—who had already paid Newcastle £330,000 for striker Malcolm Macdonald—but perhaps the shrewdest bit of business Stoke will ever do was the transfer, twice over, of striker John Ritchie. He had cost them £2,500 when they signed him from non-League football; they transferred him to Sheffield Wednesday for £75,000 . . . and re-signed him at a third of that figure. And Ritchie scored goals for Stoke during both his spells with them. His career in top-class football was finally cut short when he broke a leg.

Luton Town have had a good head for business, too—they developed and sold Bruce Rioch and Malcolm Macdonald for big fees, and got a hefty sum of money when Peter Anderson went to the Continent. They also signed the Futcher twins from Chester, for a six-figure fee, and snapped up several players with considerable First Division experience. But perhaps they wished they had hung on and waited a while, instead of letting striker Don Givens go to Queens Park Rangers for £40,000 in 1972, for this Republic of Ireland international has blossomed in skill, reputation and scoring punch to the point where he must now be rated in the £200,000 category. Still, buying and selling must always be a gamble; and, as any manager would admit, you can't win 'em all.

ANSWERS TO PAGE 21

1. Edinburgh.
2. Everton.
3. Wrexham
4. Ajax Amsterdam, and Feyenoord of Rotterdam.
5. Inter Milan, and AC Milan.
6. Brazil.
7. Real Madrid.
8. Portugal.
9. Bayern Munich.
10. Saudi Arabia.
11. Czechoslovakia beat West Germany in the Final.
12. Yugoslavia.
13. Czechoslovakia eliminated England in the Qualifying Competition.
14. Wales.
15. Duncan McKenzie.
16. The Gunners . . . Arsenal; Pompey . . . Portsmouth; The Rams . . . Derby County; The Posh . . . Peterborough United; The Hammers . . . West Ham United; The Bees . . . Brentford.
17. Composer, pianist, and singer Elton John.
18. Luton Town.
19. The first two and the last two.

20. Elland Road . . . Leeds United; St. Andrew's . . . Birmingham City; The Valley . . . Charlton Athletic; Goldstone Ground . . . Brighton; Hillsborough . . . Sheffield Wednesday; Ayresome Park . . . Middlesbrough; Filbert Street . . . Leicester City.
21. Eastville.
22. White City.
23. Manchester United and City.
24. Queen's Park.
25. North American Soccer League.
26. In 1968 as a result of a merger between the United States Association and the National Professional Soccer League.
27. Wolverhampton Wanderers...The Wolves.
28. George Best.
29. New York Cosmos.
30. Bobby Stokes.
31. 1973 Sunderland beat Leeds, 1975 Fulham lost to West Ham.
32. 1872, won by the Wanderers.
33. Liverpool Schools F.A.
34. England, beating Northern Ireland 5-0, Scotland 3-1, and drawing 1-1 with Wales.
35. Southampton.